HOW TO FORGIVE AND HEAL

The comprehensive guide to forgiving even when you don't feel like it, you can't forget or you were hurt by someone.

Michelle Brahms

EPIPHANY

Surviving a broken home and living with childhood trauma, I met Ben. He was the man who brought back my lost smile. Yes, he was much older than me, and as a young teen, many questioned why I was in a relationship with someone so much older. A 14-year age gap is often seen as inappropriate, especially when one is barely a teenager. But our relationship didn't happen overnight. It evolved from a friendship. My ignorance as a teenager, coupled with the lack of genuine parental love, left me yearning for any form of affection.

When I turned 17, my innocent friendship with Ben blossomed into love. While I poured my heart into our relationship, he seemed to be using me for his own amusement. I didn't understand the responsibilities or complexities of a relationship; I just wanted to be loved.

He further enticed me with empty promises of marriage when I turned 21. I was deeply in love, and my parents were unaware as I lived far from home after their separation. I felt like a betrothed bride, deeply bonded to him, and unable to imagine a world without him.

I built my entire world around Ben. The mere thought of him leaving was unbearable, making me feel physically ill. I mistook his small gestures—touches, smiles, shared meals, and fun conversations—as signs of true love. But I've since learned that there's a stark difference between love and mere companionship.

I left the Bahamas, where we met, to attend college in California. Ben's behavior changed drastically; he became distant, unresponsive, and uninterested. Despite my frequent visits, he grew colder, and it dawned on me that I wasn't part of his long-term plans. I realized his promises were empty, meant to control me rather than build a future together.

I persevered, even as he became harder to deal with. I needed that love and couldn't bear to see my world crumble. He was cheating on me and neglecting my feelings. My worst fear was realized when he married someone else behind my back. The betrayal caused panic attacks, and I ended up in the hospital.

It took years to heal and move on. I blamed him for a long time for his lies and for abandoning me just as I turned 21. But I eventually realized that dwelling on the past and harboring resentment only hurt me more. He was happily married with a child while I was stuck in a cycle of pain.

Forgiving him was the hardest thing I ever did, but it was essential for my healing. Forgiveness isn't about revenge or making a scene; it's about finding peace. Ben took advantage of my naivety, causing emotional breakdowns, trauma, and depression. But I wanted my peace, so I chose to forgive him, even when it seemed impossible.

Forgiveness is incredibly difficult, but when you do it for yourself, it's incredibly refreshing.

INTRODUCTION
What forgiveness can do

It frees you from the past, allowing you to move forward and reclaim your happiness.

What does forgiveness do?

Forgiveness is like setting yourself free. It's about letting go of the anger, resentment, and pain that keep you stuck in the past. It doesn't mean you're okay with what happened or that you forget about it; it's more about freeing yourself from its grip.

When you forgive, you take back control of your life. Instead of letting the hurt define you, you get to define yourself by how you heal and move forward. It's like opening a door to peace, where you can focus on your own growth and happiness.

Forgiving Ben was a tough journey. It took a lot of strength to face the pain and decide to let it go. Forgiveness wasn't about saying what he did was okay or that it didn't hurt me. It was about recognizing my own worth and deciding that his actions wouldn't control my emotions anymore.

Once I forgave him, I found a new clarity. I realized my happiness wasn't tied to him. I started to see my own strength and the courage it took to survive and heal. It showed me that I could still love and trust again, despite everything.

Forgiving also taught me empathy and compassion. I began to understand that hurt people often hurt others. While that doesn't excuse their behavior, it helped me process the pain. It allowed me to forgive myself for the mistakes I made, for the times I let my fear and longing for love cloud my judgment.

As I let go of the past, I started to build a new life. I chased my dreams, nurtured real, joyful relationships, and embraced new opportunities. The past became just a part of my story, not the whole story.

Forgiveness is really a gift you give yourself. It's about finding inner peace, emotional freedom, and room for personal growth. It's realizing you can shape your future, no matter the scars from your past. It's the ultimate act of self-care, helping you live fully and authentically.

By choosing forgiveness, you choose to live, love, and look forward to a brighter tomorrow. You reclaim your power, your story, and your heart, moving forward not as a victim of your past but as a victor in your journey.

1
Understanding Forgiveness
What Forgiveness Is and Isn't

Forgiveness is often misunderstood, so let's start by clarifying what it actually means. Forgiveness is the act of letting go of resentment and anger towards someone who has hurt you. It's about freeing yourself from the negative emotions that are tied to the past. It doesn't mean you forget what happened, excuse the behavior, or reconcile with the person who hurt you. Instead, it's a personal decision to release the hold that the hurt has over your life.

Think of forgiveness as a way to heal your own wounds. When you forgive, you're not saying that what the other person did was okay. You're simply choosing to let go of the burden of anger and pain. This can bring a sense of peace and allow you to move forward with your life.

The Psychology of Forgiveness

Understanding the psychological aspects of forgiveness can help you see why it's so important. Research shows that holding onto grudges and resentment can lead to stress, anxiety, and even physical health issues like high blood pressure and a weakened immune system. On the flip side, forgiveness can reduce stress and improve both mental and physical health.

When you forgive, your brain undergoes changes that can lead to a more positive outlook on life. It helps reduce the fight-or-flight response that keeps you in a state of stress. Instead, it activates the brain's reward system, promoting feelings of empathy, compassion, and well-being.

Common Misconceptions about Forgiveness

There are several common misconceptions about forgiveness that can make it seem more daunting than it actually is. Here are a few:

Forgiveness means forgetting: This is not true. You can forgive without forgetting. It's about releasing the emotional hold the memory has on you, not erasing the memory itself.

Forgiveness is a sign of weakness: Actually, it takes a lot of strength and courage to forgive. It's a powerful way to take control of your own emotional well-being.

You have to reconcile to forgive: Forgiveness doesn't necessarily mean you have to restore a relationship with the person who hurt you. It's about finding peace within yourself, whether or not you choose to continue a relationship.

Forgiveness happens instantly: Forgiveness is often a process that takes time. It can involve multiple steps and stages as you work through your feelings and come to terms with what happened.

Practical Steps to Understanding Forgiveness

Here are some practical steps to help you better understand and practice forgiveness:

Acknowledge your Pain: Start by acknowledging the hurt and pain you feel. Don't try to bury it or pretend it doesn't exist. Recognizing your emotions is the first step toward healing.

Reflect on the Situation: Take some time to reflect on what happened. Try to understand the context and reasons behind the other person's actions, even if it doesn't justify them. This can help you develop empathy, which is crucial for forgiveness.

Decide to Forgive: Make a conscious decision to forgive. This doesn't mean you're excusing the behavior, but you're choosing to let go of the negative emotions associated with it.

Release Resentment: Actively work on letting go of resentment and anger. This might involve talking about your feelings with a trusted friend or therapist, or practicing mindfulness and relaxation techniques.

Focus on the Present and Future: Shift your focus from the past to the present and future. Think about how you want to live your life moving forward, without being weighed down by past hurts.

Practice Self-Compassion: Be kind to yourself throughout this process. Understand that it's okay to feel hurt and that healing takes time.

If you follow these steps, you can start to understand what forgiveness really is and begin the journey toward freeing yourself from the burden of past hurts. Remember, forgiveness is not about the other person; it's about finding peace and happiness within yourself.

2
The Impact of Holding Grudges

Emotional and Physical Toll of Grudges

Holding onto grudges can have a profound impact on your emotional and physical well-being. When you cling to resentment and anger, it can cause chronic stress, which negatively affects your mental health. You might feel constantly anxious, irritable, or depressed. This emotional strain can spill over into your physical health, leading to issues like high blood pressure, heart problems, or even a weakened immune system.

Practical Steps to Release Emotional Toll

Practice Mindfulness: Engage in mindfulness meditation to become more aware of your emotions without getting overwhelmed by them.

Seek Therapy: Talking to a therapist can help you work through your feelings and develop healthier coping mechanisms.

Engage in Physical Activity: Exercise can reduce stress and improve your mood by releasing endorphins.

How Resentment Affects Relationships

Resentment can poison your relationships, both with the person you're angry at and with others around you. When you hold onto a grudge, it can create a barrier between you and the other person, making it difficult to communicate and resolve conflicts. This unresolved tension can lead to further misunderstandings and deepen the divide.

Moreover, carrying resentment can spill over into your other relationships. You might become more guarded, less trusting, and more prone to conflict with others. This can isolate you from friends and family, leaving you feeling lonely and misunderstood.

Practical Steps to Improve Relationships

Open Communication: Have honest conversations with the person you hold a grudge against, expressing your feelings calmly and clearly.

Forgiveness Letters: Write a letter to the person expressing your feelings and then choose whether to send it or not. The act of writing can be therapeutic.

Positive Interactions: Focus on building positive experiences with others to counterbalance the negativity from holding grudges.

The Cost of Living in the Past

When you hold a grudge, you are essentially living in the past. You constantly replay the hurtful event in your mind, which prevents you from fully engaging in the present. This can stifle your personal growth and keep you from experiencing joy and new opportunities.

Living in the past also prevents you from moving forward. You might find it hard to set new goals or pursue new interests because you're so focused on what happened before. This can create a sense of stagnation and dissatisfaction in your life.

Practical Steps to Embrace the Present

Set New Goals: Focus on what you want to achieve in the future rather than what happened in the past.

Mindful Living: Practice being present in the moment, appreciating the here and now rather than dwelling on past hurts.

Gratitude Journal: Keep a journal where you write down things you're grateful for each day. This shifts your focus from past grievances to present blessings.

Holding grudges can significantly impact your emotional and physical health, harm your relationships, and keep you trapped in the past. By acknowledging these effects and taking practical steps to let go of resentment, you can improve your overall well-being and open yourself up to a more positive, fulfilling future. Remember, forgiveness is not about excusing the wrongs done to you but about freeing yourself from their control.

3
Self-Reflection and Awareness
Recognizing Your Pain

To forgive, you first need to understand and acknowledge your pain. Ignoring or burying your feelings won't make them go away. Take time to sit quietly and reflect on what happened. Ask yourself questions like: What exactly hurt me? Why does it hurt so much? How has this pain affected my life? Writing down your thoughts can help clarify your emotions and bring hidden feelings to the surface.

Practical Steps

Journaling: Write about the incident and how it made you feel. Describe your emotions in detail.

Meditation: Spend a few minutes each day in quiet reflection. Focus on your breath and gently bring your mind back to the pain you're feeling.

Talking It Out: Share your feelings with a trusted friend or therapist. Sometimes, verbalizing your pain helps you understand it better.

Understanding Your Emotions

Once you've recognized your pain, it's essential to delve deeper into your emotions. Understand that feeling hurt, angry, or sad is normal. These emotions are natural responses to being wronged. Allow yourself to feel these emotions without judgment. Realize that your feelings are valid and important.

Practical Steps

Emotion Mapping: Write down each emotion you're feeling and explore why you feel that way.

Self-Compassion: Treat yourself with kindness and acknowledge that it's okay to feel hurt.

Mindfulness: Practice being present with your emotions without trying to change them. Notice how they feel in your body and mind.

Identifying the Source of Your Hurt

Pinpointing the exact source of your hurt is crucial. It might be a specific action, a series of events, or a betrayal of trust. Sometimes, the hurt can be compounded by past experiences. Reflect on whether the pain is solely from the current situation or if it's also bringing up old wounds.

Practical Steps

Timeline Exercise: Create a timeline of events leading up to and following the hurtful incident. This can help you see patterns and identify triggers.

Root Cause Analysis: Ask yourself "why" several times. For example, "Why does this hurt me?" Answer, then ask "Why is that?" and continue until you reach the root cause.

Past vs. Present: Distinguish between current hurts and old wounds. Acknowledge if past experiences are influencing your current emotions.

By engaging in self-reflection and becoming more aware of your pain, emotions, and their sources, you lay a strong foundation for forgiveness. Understanding your pain and where it comes from is the first step towards letting it go. This chapter is not about rushing through your feelings but about genuinely understanding and processing them. The more clarity you have about your pain, the better equipped you are to move towards forgiveness.

Next Steps

Now that you have a clearer understanding of your pain and emotions, the next chapter will guide you through the steps to forgive others. Remember, forgiveness is a journey. Take your time, be kind to yourself, and stay open to healing.

4
Steps to Forgive Others

Forgiving someone who has hurt you can be one of the most challenging things to do. This chapter will guide you through the steps to forgive others, helping you to release the burden of resentment and move toward healing and peace. Each step includes practical advice and exercises to support you on your journey.

Acknowledging the Hurt

The first step in forgiving someone is acknowledging the hurt they caused you. Denying or minimizing your pain can prevent you from truly healing.

Practical Steps

Reflect on Your Feelings: Take some quiet time to think about what happened and how it made you feel. Write down your thoughts in a journal.

Be Honest with Yourself: Accept that you are hurt. It's okay to feel pain, anger, or sadness.

Understanding the Offender's Perspective

Trying to understand why the person hurt you can help you to see the situation from a different angle. This doesn't mean you're excusing their behavior, but it can help you find some empathy.

Practical Steps

Consider Their Situation: Think about what might have led them to act the way they did. Were they dealing with their own issues or pain?

Ask Questions: If possible and appropriate, talk to the person and ask them why they behaved as they did. This can provide insights that you hadn't considered.

Finding Empathy and Compassion

Empathy involves putting yourself in the other person's shoes and trying to feel what they felt. Compassion is about recognizing their humanity and imperfections.

Practical Steps

Practice Empathy Exercises: Imagine being in their situation and feeling what they felt. This can help you understand their actions better.

Use Affirmations: Repeat to yourself phrase like, "I choose to understand and forgive," or "I release the burden of anger."

Letting Go of Resentment

Holding onto resentment keeps you trapped in a cycle of negativity. Letting go is essential for your own peace of mind.

Practical Steps

Visualize Releasing the Hurt: Close your eyes and imagine the pain and anger leaving your body. See it float away like a balloon.

Mindfulness Meditation: Practice mindfulness to stay in the present moment and detach from lingering negative feelings.

Communicating Your Forgiveness

Once you feel ready, communicating your forgiveness to the person can be a powerful step. It can bring closure and help both parties move forward.

Practical Steps

Write a Letter: If you can't or don't want to speak to the person directly, write them a letter. You don't have to send it; the act of writing can be therapeutic.

Have a Conversation: If you feel comfortable, have a calm and open conversation with the person. Express your feelings and let them know you forgive them.

Putting It All Together

Forgiving others is a process that takes time and effort. It involves acknowledging your hurt, understanding the other person's perspective, finding empathy and compassion, letting go of resentment, and, if possible, communicating your forgiveness. Each step brings you closer to healing and peace.

Remember, forgiveness is not about excusing the behavior or forgetting what happened. It's about freeing yourself from the emotional burden and finding a way to move forward with your life.

Practical Exercise

Daily Forgiveness Practice: Every day, take a few minutes to reflect on any lingering negative feelings towards others. Use the steps outlined above to work through these feelings, and remind yourself of the peace that comes with forgiveness.

By following these steps, you can start to release the weight of past hurts and open yourself up to a future filled with peace, happiness, and healthier relationships.P a g e | 25

5
Forgiving Yourself

Forgiving yourself is just as important as forgiving others. Often, the hardest person to forgive is yourself. This chapter will guide you through understanding the necessity of self-forgiveness, overcoming guilt and shame, the steps to achieve self-forgiveness, and embracing self-compassion.

The Importance of Self-Forgiveness

Self-forgiveness is crucial for your mental and emotional well-being. Holding onto self-blame and guilt can weigh you down and prevent you from moving forward. It's important to recognize that everyone makes mistakes and that these mistakes don't define your worth.

When you forgive yourself, you allow yourself to grow from your experiences rather than be defined by them. Self-forgiveness helps you build a healthier relationship with yourself, fostering self-respect and inner peace.

Overcoming Guilt and Shame

Guilt and shame are powerful emotions that can hold you back. Guilt is the feeling of remorse for something you've done, while shame is the feeling that you are inherently flawed because of your actions. Overcoming these emotions is essential to forgiving yourself.

Acknowledge Your Feelings: The first step is to acknowledge your feelings of guilt and shame. Don't suppress them; instead, face them head-on.

Understand the Source: Identify why you feel guilty or ashamed. Understanding the root cause can help you address it more effectively.

Challenge Negative Thoughts: Often, we exaggerate our mistakes and the consequences. Challenge these negative thoughts by putting things in perspective.

Talk About It: Sharing your feelings with a trusted friend or therapist can help you process your emotions and gain a different perspective.

Steps to Self-Forgiveness

Forgiving yourself involves several steps that require introspection and commitment. Here's how you can start:

Accept Responsibility: Acknowledge what you did wrong. Accepting responsibility is crucial to moving forward.

2. **Make Amends**: If possible, try to make amends with those you may have hurt. Apologize sincerely and make an effort to rectify your mistakes.

Learn from the Experience: Reflect on what you've learned from the situation. Understanding the lesson can prevent you from making the same mistake again.

Practice Self-Compassion: Treat yourself with the same kindness you would offer a friend. Understand that being imperfect is part of being human.

Let Go of Perfectionism: Accept that you cannot be perfect. Striving for perfection only leads to disappointment and self-criticism.

Embracing Self-Compassion

Self-compassion is about being kind to yourself, especially during times of failure or suffering. It involves treating yourself with the same care and understanding you would offer to others.

Mindfulness: Be aware of your feelings without judgment. Recognize your pain and accept it without letting it overwhelm you.

Self-Kindness: Talk to yourself in a gentle, encouraging way. Instead of harsh criticism, offer words of comfort and support.

Common Humanity: Remember that everyone makes mistakes and experiences difficulties. You are not alone in your struggles.

Practical Steps for Self-Forgiveness

To make self-forgiveness a part of your daily life, try these practical steps:

Daily Affirmations: Start your day with positive affirmations. Remind yourself of your worth and your capacity to grow.

Journaling: Write down your thoughts and feelings. Reflecting on paper can help you process your emotions and see your growth.

Meditation: Practice mindfulness meditation to center yourself and reduce negative self-talk.

Seek Support: Don't hesitate to seek support from friends, family, or a professional counselor. Talking things out can provide clarity and comfort.

Set Realistic Goals: Set achievable goals for yourself. Celebrate your progress, no matter how small.

6
Practical Strategies for Forgiveness

Forgiveness isn't always easy, but there are practical strategies that can help you navigate this challenging journey. In this chapter, we'll explore some simple yet effective techniques to help you forgive yourself and others.

Mindfulness and Meditation Techniques

Mindfulness and meditation can be powerful tools for cultivating forgiveness. By practicing mindfulness, you can learn to observe your thoughts and emotions without judgment, which can help you let go of resentment and anger. Meditation techniques such as loving-kindness meditation can also help you cultivate feelings of compassion and empathy towards yourself and others.

Practical Step

Set aside a few minutes each day to practice mindfulness meditation. Find a quiet space, close your eyes, and focus on your breath. As thoughts arise, simply observe them without getting caught up in them. Repeat a mantra such as "May I forgive myself and others" to cultivate feelings of forgiveness and compassion.

Journaling and Expressive Writing

Journaling and expressive writing can be therapeutic tools for processing emotions and gaining clarity on past experiences. By writing about your feelings, you can gain insight into your thoughts and behaviors and begin to release pent-up emotions. You can also use journaling prompts to explore forgiveness and reflect on ways to let go of grudges.

Practical Step

Set aside time each day to write in a journal. Start by writing about a specific situation or person that you're struggling to forgive. Write freely and without judgment, allowing your thoughts and emotions to flow onto the page. Notice any patterns or insights that arise as you write.

Cognitive Behavioral Approaches

Cognitive-behavioral approaches can help you challenge negative thought patterns and beliefs that may be contributing to your inability to forgive. By identifying and reframing distorted thinking, you can begin to see the situation from a new perspective and let go of resentments. Cognitive-behavioral techniques such as cognitive restructuring and thought stopping can help you break free from rumination and self-blame.

Practical Step

Keep a thought record to track your negative thoughts and beliefs about forgiveness. Whenever you notice yourself engaging in negative self-talk or blaming others, challenge these thoughts by asking yourself questions such as "Is this thought helpful?" and "What evidence do I have to support this belief?" Replace negative thoughts with more balanced and compassionate statements.

Seeking Professional Help

Sometimes, forgiveness can be a complex and challenging process that may require professional support. A therapist or counselor can provide you with guidance and support as you navigate your feelings and work towards forgiveness. They can help you explore underlying issues, develop coping strategies, and process difficult emotions in a safe and supportive environment.

7

Rebuilding Trust and Relationships
Setting Healthy Boundaries

Rebuilding trust begins with setting healthy boundaries. Boundaries are essential for protecting yourself and ensuring that the same hurtful behavior doesn't happen again. They help you define what is acceptable and what isn't in your relationships.

Practical Steps

Identify Your Boundaries: Think about what behaviors are unacceptable and what you need to feel safe and respected.

Communicate Clearly: Once you know your boundaries, communicate them clearly to the person involved. Be honest and direct about your needs and expectations.

Be Consistent: Stick to your boundaries consistently. If they are crossed, address the issue immediately to reinforce their importance.

Respect Others' Boundaries: Just as you have your own boundaries, respect those of others. Healthy relationships are built on mutual respect.

Re-establishing Communication

Effective communication is key to rebuilding trust. Without open and honest dialogue, misunderstandings and resentments can fester, making it difficult to move forward.

Practical Steps

Be Honest: Share your feelings and thoughts openly. Honesty is crucial for rebuilding trust.

Listen Actively: Pay attention to what the other person is saying without interrupting. Show that you value their perspective.

Use "I" Statements: Focus on expressing your feelings and needs without blaming the other person. For example, say "I feel hurt when..." instead of "You hurt me by..."

Stay Calm: Keep emotions in check during difficult conversations. Take breaks if needed to cool down and gather your thoughts.

The Role of Time and Patience

Rebuilding trust takes time. It won't happen overnight, and it requires patience from both parties. Understand that healing is a process, and allow yourself and the other person time to rebuild the relationship gradually.

Practical Steps

Be Patient: Understand that trust-building is a slow process. Give it the time it needs without rushing.

Show Consistency: Consistent behavior over time helps rebuild trust. Be reliable and dependable.

Celebrate Small Wins: Acknowledge and celebrate small steps toward rebuilding trust. This reinforces positive progress.

Practice Forgiveness: Be willing to forgive minor setbacks as long as there is a genuine effort to improve.

When to Reconcile and When to Move On

Not every relationship can or should be reconciled. Sometimes, the healthiest choice is to move on. Understanding when to continue rebuilding and when to let go is crucial for your well-being.

Practical Steps

Assess the Relationship: Consider if the relationship adds value to your life and if the other person is genuinely trying to change.

Look for Effort: Reconciliation should be mutual. If the other person isn't putting in the effort, it may be time to move on.

Trust You're Gut: Listen to your instincts. If something feels wrong, it might be a sign that reconciliation isn't the best option.

Seek Support: Talk to trusted friends, family, or a therapist for advice. Sometimes an outside perspective can help you make the right decision.

Rebuilding trust and relationships is challenging but rewarding. By setting healthy boundaries, re-establishing communication, being patient, and knowing when to reconcile or move on, you can create stronger, healthier connections. Remember, trust is built over time with consistent effort and mutual respect. Keep these steps in mind as you navigate the path to rebuilding trust, and you will find yourself on a journey toward deeper, more meaningful relationships.

8
Personal Stories of Forgiveness

In this aspect, I will share some personal short stories in my therapy sessions and proceed to helping see why forgiveness is essential.

Forgiveness Stories of forgiveness are significant and powerful. It can be the balm for battle scars, the peace treaty between warring neighbors, or the light at the end of the tunnel. But what exactly is forgiveness in practice? These stories show forgiveness despite the unimaginable situations they represent, inspiring us with the impactful vision of what this forgiveness means and can teach us. Coming up on the page are real life therapy result stories about how letting go can empower you.

Inspiring Stories of Forgiveness

The Power of Letting Go (from Lisa)

I'm Lisa and my sister, Jessica, had always been close. But a bitter dispute over a family inheritance led to a falling out between us. For years, there was no communication, the pain of betrayal still fresh. The burden was much and I did not want to carry this burden any longer, and one day I messaged Jessica, because the silence was getting boring. For hours— we sat down, met, talked, cried, and forgave each other. Cutting our losses had helped us more than they could have ever imagined, demonstrating that forgiveness is the ultimate cornerstone of rekindling a broken relationship.

A Father's Love without Condition (from Samuel)

I was heartbroken when his son, Tony was involved in a crime and ended up in prison. Shame and disappointment were so thick our relationship was on the rocks. Despite my feelings, i visited Tony every week, making sure Tony felt loved and cared for. Eventually, I fight to forgive him because he is my blood and I have only him, gradually I see that my effort to show love despite disappointment caused Tony to change his life. When Tony was released from prison, he got his life together.

Forgiving the Unforgivable (From Adrian)

Adrian's story is one of the most powerful parts of the book. A dangerous assault leaves him both physically and emotionally scared. The idea of forgiving his assaulter, Maxwell, seemed inconceivable. Yet Adrian came to forgive, with the help of our therapists and support. He was filled with of guilt and anger, and this was what kept him from being who he wanted to be, so for him, this forgiveness was not about justifying that crime but forgiving him from that anger and pain. Adrian's journey out of his misery shows that forgiveness can lead to self-healing even when one is heavily justified.

What We Learn from Real-Life Stories

It Takes Time to Forgive

Forgiveness just doesn't happen. It is not a light switch on and off—often involving time, reflection, and sometimes professional assistance. For some, it may be the path to repairing a relationship with a family member; for others, it may be an avenue for overcoming personal trauma.

The Power of Forgiveness

Forgiveness can really go a long way in how it affects your daily life. It helps us in dropping negative emotions, it cuts down stress, and it is beneficial for our mental health. Forgiveness is a critical part of moving through deep trauma, as in Adrian's case.

The Ripple Effect of Forgiveness

Forgiving someone isn't just powerful for the person who forgives; it also impacts those around them. Samuel's forgiveness managed to turn his son's life around, which shows just how far-reaching a simple act of forgiveness can be for the better of all.

It requires a lot of courage and strength to be forgiving. The underlying message of these stories is that forgiveness is not a sign of weakness or an endorsement of wrong behavior, it is about moving on. The moral of the story of Lisa and Jessica provides hope through forgiveness to strengthen relationships and a more fully formed empathy and relationship with another.

My forgiveness journey personal anecdotes revealing the power of it. They remind us of the courage in forgiveness because to forgive is a brave deed; it heals, it mends, and it invokes a deeply profound sense of peace. In our own lives, these stories can aid us as lighthouses, showing us the way to forgiveness, the path of liberation and healing.

Conclusion

It is such a transforming, deep journey—almost courageous in the face of time—and a yearning for healing that throbs through. For healing, what we could gather from this book is that forgiving is by no means pardoning actions that have inflicted hurt or forgetting them. Instead, this frees you from the heavy load of anger, resentment, and pain. It will give you back your peace, after which you can move forward with a light heart.

The reflection from your journey of forgiveness lets you realize you have grown, with so much resilience in you. Every step taken to establish healthy boundaries, build empathy, and re-establish communication brings one step closer to walking free and living a tranquil life. Acceptance of forgiveness only purports acceptance of one's well-being and choice of living without chains of past pains.

And much like all the other intentions you put in place, you will realize that forgiveness is a journey walked out every day of your life. It is not a destination; it is the journey in life's evolution that you sprout with. It will be a struggle, and I am sure there will be moments of doubt for sure. but in that forgiving, you strengthen the ability to live an inspired life where compassion and understanding are rife. Surround yourself with people who support you, get inspiration from other people's stories, and just reflect on the progress you have made.

Forgiveness changes the heart, heals relationships, and cures almost everything. It changes the way you see life such that you begin to accept stronger connections and more emotional health, as well as a future untainted by the past. This is self-love through the acts of the bravest and boldest hearts. So, continue to forgive, continue to heal, and keep on moving. Your journey is unique, and your capability of forgiveness is limitless. Take up and embrace fully the power of forgiveness. All that comes with forgiveness is always a life of peace, happiness, and freedom.

Bonus
Forgiveness Exercises and Worksheets

Introduction to Forgiveness
Define Forgiveness

1. What does forgiveness mean to you?

2. How do you feel when you think about forgiving someone?

Benefits of Forgiveness

List the Benefits

1. List at least five benefits of forgiveness.

2. Reflect on how these benefits can improve your life.

Misconceptions about Forgiveness
Common Misconceptions

1. Identify common misconceptions about forgiveness (e.g., "Forgiving means forgetting," "Forgiveness is a sign of weakness").

2. Write down why these misconceptions are false and what the truth is.

Reflection on Forgiveness
Personal Reflection Prompts

Personal Forgiveness Reflection

1. Think of a time when you forgave someone. How did it feel?

2. Think of a time when you struggled to forgive. What were the barriers?

Identifying Grudges and Resentments
Exercise: Grudge List

1. Make a list of people or situations you are holding grudges against.

2. For each item, write down how it affects you and what it would mean to let go.

Empathy Building

49

Empathy Exercises

Exercise: *Walking in Their Shoes*

1. Choose a person you need to forgive. Write a paragraph from their perspective about the situation.

Understanding the Other Person's Perspective

Perspective-Taking

1. What might have motivated their actions?

2. What might they have been feeling at the time?

Forgiveness Techniques

Letter Writing Exercise

Worksheet: Forgiveness Letter

1. Recipient: Who are you writing this letter to?

2. Opening: Start by addressing the person and acknowledging the situation.

3. Express Your Feelings: Write about how the situation affected you emotionally, mentally, and physically.

4. State Your Intentions: Clearly state that you are choosing to forgive them. Explain why this decision is important to you.

5. Close with Compassion: End the letter on a positive note, expressing hope for the future and any final thoughts.

Guided Imagery and Visualization

Exercise: Visualization Practice

1. Sit comfortably and close your eyes. Visualize a peaceful place and imagine a scenario where you forgive the person.

Self-Compassion Practices

Exercise: Self-Compassion Letter

1. Write a letter to yourself expressing understanding and compassion for your own pain.

Forgiveness in Action
Forgiveness Plan

Worksheet: Creating a Forgiveness Plan

1. Identify one person you are ready to forgive.

2. Outline steps you will take to forgive them (e.g., having a conversation, writing a letter).

Role-Playing Scenarios

Exercise: Forgiveness Role-Play

1. With a partner, role-play a forgiveness conversation. One person plays themselves, and the other plays the person they need to forgive.

<table>
<tr><td>

</td></tr>
<tr><td>

</td></tr>
</table>

Maintaining Forgiveness
Daily Affirmations
Worksheet: Forgiveness Affirmations

1. Create a list of affirmations that reinforce forgiveness (e.g., "I release anger and choose peace").

<table>
<tr><td>
</td></tr>
<tr><td>
</td></tr>
<tr><td>
</td></tr>
<tr><td>
</td></tr>
<tr><td>
</td></tr>
<tr><td>
</td></tr>
<tr><td>
</td></tr>
<tr><td>
</td></tr>
</table>

Gratitude Practices

Exercise: Gratitude Journal

1. Each day, write down three things you are grateful for. Reflect on how forgiveness has impacted your gratitude.

(get an empty journal book for a longer space to write)

Journaling for Continued Reflection

Worksheet: Forgiveness Journal

1. Keep a journal dedicated to your forgiveness journey. Write regular entries about your progress, challenges, and feelings.

(Get an empty journal for a longer space to write)

Example Worksheet: Forgiveness Letter
Forgiveness Letter Worksheet

1. Recipient:

Who are you writing this letter to?

2. Opening:

Start by addressing the person and acknowledging the situation.

3. Express your Feelings:

Write about how the situation affected you emotionally, mentally, and physically.

4. State Your Intentions:

Clearly state that you are choosing to forgive them. Explain why this decision is important to you.

5. Close with Compassion:

End the letter on a positive note, expressing hope for the future and any final thoughts.

THE END

www.ingramcontent.com/pod-product-compliance
Lightning Source LLC
Chambersburg PA
CBHW051850250726
48659CB00006B/2122